## Praise for *The Venus of Odesa*

Compassion and irony define the human predicaments and historical conditions in Askold Melnyczuk's extraordinary new collection of poems that spans nearly fifty years. His cosmopolitan perspective—one that twines Ukraine and New England—probes time and death, and the relationship between the tragic and the comic with a nimble wit that humanizes. These poems shake you up in the most important ways that poetry can.

—Peter Balakian, author of *Ozone Journal*,
winner of the Pulitzer Prize for poetry

When I heard that Askold Melnyczuk had finally collected his poetry written over the past fifty years, I thought, *High time!* Now those who know him as a superb fiction writer, a tireless advocate for Ukrainian and American writers, a publisher who publishes books for the sole reason that he loves them, and a gentle scoffer at all things/people/causes that are bloated on their own self-importance, will get to see yet another side of his literary genius. As lyrical in feeling as they are rigorously made, these poems are a brave and bracing attempt, in Yeats's phrase, "to hold reality and justice in a single thought." At the same time, he knows that his father seeing a rose window in a yogurt cup or a refugee losing his teeth on the ship to so-called "freedom" can't be shrugged off as epiphenomena, the merely personal, the clod-consciousness of "a potato reading Rilke." Wised up, amused, disabused, deeply felt, these poems have always taken the potato's side, the side that stays rooted in the earth no matter what self-righteous abstractions or large-scale truths seem to hold sway at any given moment. Grounded in history, in atrocity, and in a rare sweetness and generosity, his poems are the exuberant record of a truly humane way of being in the world.

—Tom Sleigh, author of *The King's Touch*

*The Venus of Odesa*, Askold Melnyczuk's new and selected poems, is both a debut collection and the harvest of a lifetime. Youthful and wise, intimate yet eternal in voice, he is a keen recorder of the sweep of history as well as the sweep-hand of time's layered implications. In "The Enamel Box," he writes; "I imagine / a mother, a father, a child a house: / eternal actors, paramours of joy and pain, / except the child, born all eyes, / who sits at the window / watching dragonflies / and does not know / centuries are passing. / This is how they pass." Sometimes rueful, sometimes stinging, always deeply humane, these poems of heritage, family, and friendship are dear to the heart as they toll the heartbeat of our moment. Askold Melnyczuk is among the best poets of his generation.

—Stuart Dischell, author of *The Lookout Man*

# THE VENUS OF ODESA

*Poems: New and Selected*

# THE VENUS OF ODESA
*Poems: New and Selected*

Askold Melnyczuk

MadHat Press
Cheshire, Massachusetts

MadHat Press
MadHat Incorporated
PO Box 422, Cheshire, MA 01225

Copyright © 2025 Askold Melnyczuk
All rights reserved.

The Library of Congress has assigned
this edition a Control Number of
2025936970

ISBN 978-1-952335-97-6 (paperback)

Words by Askold Melnyczuk
Cover image: untitled © 2024 by Ksenia Datsiuk
(oil on paper)
Cover design by Marc Vincenz

www.MadHat-Press.com

First Printing
Printed in the United States of America

*for Helen, Christine and Lara*

# Table of Contents

| | |
|---|---:|
| Dance of the Tomahawks | 1 |

### I

| | |
|---|---:|
| The Sunday Before Easter | 5 |
| And So | 10 |
| Forsythia | 11 |
| The Way of the World | 12 |
| The Usual Immigrant Uncle Poem | 13 |
| The Mouth Refuses to Translate | 14 |
| The Voyagers | 15 |
| One Image Crossed the Many-headed | 17 |
| A Potato Reading Rilke | 18 |
| The Enamel Box | 20 |
| My Father Has a Vision | 22 |
| Geese in Winter, Medford | 23 |
| Questions I Never Asked My Father | 24 |
| Chorale: *In April* | 25 |

### II

| | |
|---|---:|
| Late | 29 |
| De Tocqueville in Newark | 32 |
| La Bohème | 34 |
| Poets' Loves | 38 |
| From the Streets | 39 |
| Head | 45 |
| The Odyssey, Revised, Standard | 46 |
| On a Painting by Edward Kozak | 47 |
| Simplon Pass | 48 |
| I.E., | 49 |
| Sweet Enough | 50 |
| My Life Against the Berlin Wall | 54 |

| | |
|---|---|
| The Cost of Nothing | 57 |
| Metamorphosis | 58 |
| Nobody's Right | 60 |
| The Light Around You | 61 |
| Haruspicating Clouds in Cambridge | 63 |
| Alley Cat | 65 |
| The Great Feeding | 67 |
| Poem | 68 |
| Goya's Winter | 69 |
| Melancholy Baby | 72 |
| Prayer of Origin | 74 |
| After a Snowfall the Second Day of Spring | 76 |
| Cambridge Typewriter Is Now In Arlington | 77 |

### III. Personae

| | |
|---|---|
| Girl in the Prado | 81 |
| The Revelations of Julius Caesar | 84 |
| Descartes: Final Notes | 86 |
| Dear Liv Ullman, I Hope You Are Never Unhappy | 87 |
| Swan Song | 88 |

### IV. Versions from the Ukrainian

| | |
|---|---|
| Three Fables by Hrihory Skovoroda | 93 |
| Five by Taras Shevchenko | 96 |
| War by Pavlo Tychyna | 103 |
| Two by Mykola Rudenko | 104 |
| Two by Marjana Savka | 107 |

### V.

| | |
|---|---|
| Vermont | 113 |
| Downer Forest Road | 114 |
| Buddhist Diary: 1954–2024 | 116 |
| The Great Blue Heron | 117 |
| A Trophy of Shadows | 119 |

| | |
|---|---|
| Who | 120 |
| In the Arms of the World | 122 |
| Portrait of Lucie at Stop and Shop | 124 |
| The Other Lives | 125 |
| All Talk Is Moths | 128 |
| The Venus of Odesa | 129 |
| Verses from Shantideva | 132 |
| | |
| *Big Thanks* | 135 |
| *Acknowledgments* | 137 |
| *About the Author* | 139 |

*Men hep tavas a golas y dyr:*
The tongueless man gets his land took.

—Tony Harrison

# Dance of the Tomahawks

The Tomahawks are pushing icepicks
Through my teeth—I'm seeing stars
I think my luck is changing for the better
Snap of sinews, knee to chest, toe to groin
How long I've longed to bleed internally

Lying flat on this dark street
I watch the young chief rub his hands together
He is thinking of his mother
Whose hair he wears
Whose eyes he has

He falls to his knees
Roots them firmly in my pelvic cushion
And raises his hands to the sky
His hot tears mingle with mine like a garland
And

We know
We are brothers one
Soul continually searching
Each in his manner
Each in his manner

*1974*

The Tomahawks were a Brooklyn street gang active in the seventies.

# I.

*And everywhere it was my America, and I didn't know it.*

# The Sunday Before Easter

> *Dreadful it is*
> *How here and there*
> *Endlessly God disperses*
> *Whatever lives.*
> —Holderlin

**1**

I prayed each twilight with the crickets
as a boy to another boy, rapt
in his mother's blue-gowned arms:

*Otche Nash.*

Concentration is prayer;
Poetry the private psalm.

Sunday before Easter
before dawn revives
the city with its debonair
starlings, startled by weather

to wooing, behind
my desk, from where
in the window I can see your double
I pray the only way I can.

I tell you my stories
because they are mysteries,

Askold Melnyczuk

## 2

because
the little god who dwells within,
reflecting God, creating
worlds with names, remembers.

My country, formerly the sun
became the oil-slicked water;
sapped pine barrens and barren
suburbia;

the "Venice of New Jersey"
since it flooded every year;
at times, mountains
and ignitable, polluted air

feel familiar
as the silk of your bed,

the blue-gold silk of your breasts.

## 3

Lviv, Peremyshl, Berchtesgaden:
there God flared in
his latest conflagration, disguised
in brown, or agonized
green;

## The Venus of Odesa

booted, buckled,
moustache trim, chin
shaved clean as an apple,

proud of himself,
his shining discipline,
the moral courage to shelve
tobacco, moonlight, women.

He puffed himself especially
on his talent for division,
like that evolutionary
wonder, the amoeba;

for rising early, spitting
in his own glum sun,
showering in splinters
of ice-water without wincing,

marching in unison
with himself, raising legs
muscled as if modeled by Rodin.

And he was proud
of his spired libraries
outstripping Alexandria

where the dead speak, and the living are silent.

*Askold Melnyczuk*

He visited a museum
ransomed by lions,
accompanied by an interpreter
from the far city of Babel.

God torched houses.
He castrated boys, inspired
women burning for food
to murder their husbands.

He turned his people back to light.
I saw none of this,

but I remember.

4

I remember and rehearse it
for you—who else
could balance the scales
of justice?

These fairy tales mother
lent me for lullabies.
What once delivered me to sleep
now keeps me up

long after the emaciated hands
of the clock unclasp

The Venus of Odesa

and splay to quarter-cross
and the cat, and you, sleep.

*Askold Melnyczuk*

# And So

amid the loved lost causes,
the revival of the classics,
the classless society

you work on a dirge
for the language
your grandmother loved you in:

*snih, trava, lyubov*

# Forsythia

and pussy willows feather
framed Madonnas. I stand

on a dining-room table
like a lamp reciting
syllables of unbroken light

by a poet a century gone—
what fine filaments burned
whenever I forgot myself.

Mother stitches a pillow,
nodding her strawberry head.
A tipped oak rankles the window.

Years later, I enter a room
brightened by bolts of forsythia
and see the prophetic scythe

of the peasant, and a black horse
calmly threading the wind

into the cold, white blouse of the steppes.

*Askold Melnyczuk*

# The Way of the World

*December, 1980*

Reading Duns Scotus, I find
this passage, a quotation
from Avicenna:
Those who deny
a first principle
should be beaten
or exposed to fire until
they concede that to burn
and not to burn
or to be beaten
and not to be beaten
are not identical.

The Soviet Army masses
at the Polish border.
Larry Lee, a living soul,
is in Seattle.
He is singing.
Later tonight I'll read poems
by Rudenko, who is in prison
for speaking out for the beaten.
Later still,
Heraclitus
on war, fire, and change.

# The Usual Immigrant Uncle Poem

He feared money so much he was known
to shake and sweat in line at the register.

Once, they say, he broke down and wept.
And it seemed funny to us at Christmas

when he wore
his sister-in-law's underwear

on his head.
But we did not know

how it had been
back in Pereyaslav

or whatever other place
I never saw, and so

can't care for, really,
where they took his father,

a famous judge and orator
and stood him against the wall

and so on. Still,
that doesn't quite explain the money.

*Askold Melnyczuk*

# The Mouth Refuses to Translate

I think *serce moyeh*
but what I say
my pen won't put
to paper in

this hostile tongue—
this Jacob's ladder
I am testing
rung by rung.

# The Voyagers

*for Peter*

*The bottom of the sea is cruel.*
    —Hart Crane

**1**

Each week
they meet to rehearse

The Losing of the Teeth.
On the boat coming over

he brooded
the apotropaic water.

Sea of Withdrawal.
Sea of Deep Breathing.

Body, suffer
a sea change.

When his dentures
dropped out,

his wife screamed:
"Part of a man

overboard."
The sailors

spat
and ignored her.

2

He survived.
They arrived.

Settled.
Smiled shyly.

Made their way
out of the ghetto

into the burbs.
Children, money, sunflowers.

But what he knew
he kept to himself,

gaping nightly
at the half-empty glass,

fingering his jaw
(a fair fit):

that no man willingly ever
gave up his teeth.

# One Image Crossed the Many-Headed

You look in the mirror,
that history book,
and cut yourself shaving.

That summer
stars stoked the wind,
spiraling petals like ash.

If telling the story once
made the undivided country
open underfoot, if saying it

once brought peace,
you would gladly
turn to the lilacs,

her eyes,
all the night
green, and blooming.

*Askold Melnyczuk*

# A Potato Reading Rilke

Suddenly the crap has meaning:
old wallets, scarves, the radio
years in a drawer, batteries, blue
shirt, the almost new
sweaters, the scarred belts.

Apocatastasis of objects!
Someone else will one day squirm
inside the suit from Syms
your father bought you
for some funeral, or wedding.

To this day you've been
a potato reading Rilke,
skipping every other word
to get the moral at the end,
a morsel of meaning

you could mouth
like a seduction song your spirit
needed, lost inside
the jazz of lights, the stop
and go, with clouds hallucinating

rain and dirt and the poor,
a key to how to walk
into a bookstore or a bar.
The walls heard you all
too often, the air

aged with you.
Still the centripetal flower,
the secret presence
planted in the heart
of our life's decay

argues with Trotsky who
like all prophets, loved
the future tense too much:
this is not lies.
Matter dreaming finds

a sweetness light permits
its sickest kids.
And he: Yeah, sure.
But the junk in your closet
rises like Lazarus because

those on this planet have needs
you can answer.
Pack your suitcase, green
nylon, from Spain, pack it
full of that

manufactured ego,
and go.

Askold Melnyczuk

# The Enamel Box

> Given my mother by a visitor from Ukraine

It was a country and a house
I'd never seen.
This trinket and odd record of humanity,
starfish, pewter, purple, green—
ancestral garden from a greener age—
and I turn outward to the oak which spring
has, like a famished lover, licked
awake.

I imagine
somewhere beyond the tree
that house, the solitary, careful
child within,
and the dragonflies
rising and falling like pistons
above a sputtering stream.

The mother bakes bread by an open
window, humming softly to a dying sun.
The father smokes a pipe, instructs the child:
"Cultivate wheat and a conscience.
In a pinch, forfeit
the conscience
but save that wheat."

It jars me, this lecture
I've imagined, because
there ought to be causes
worth dying for,

THE VENUS OF ODESA

and my peasant says no.
Is it the mysteries of Eleusis
he's understood, while I

battling each morning uncharitable
Aristotle,
worry the fine points,
obscure to the whole?

The old man says to the boy:
"Anyone tells you God cares
about anything except kindness
is a liar."

I imagine
a mother, a father, a child, a house:
eternal actors, paramours of joy and pain,
except the child, born all eyes,
who sits at the window
watching the dragonflies
and does not know
centuries are passing.

This is how they pass.

*Askold Melnyczuk*

# My Father Has a Vision

A cathedral rose
In a pint of yoghurt
You were spooning.

Look! You cried. Look!
I raced in from the other room, fearing
You'd fallen. Look, you cried,

What's it doing there?
And, truly, father,
A gray stone spire

Probed the air
Draped in white silk
Above the eight-ounce cup

Supported by flying buttresses,
A rose window, snarling
Gargoyles spouting fire.

It wasn't the morphine.
You weren't dying of pain. You saw
What you saw.

And the pigeons exploded
Into the room and roosted
Above your bed.

# Geese in Winter, Medford

Serene, the geese refuse my offered bread.
They look at me and quickly turn away,
their long necks plundering the riverbed
below. Aquatic gardens rise and sway,
feeding restless pilgrims on their way

to somewhere I have never travelled.
My father, dying, said: I never willed
harm on a single soul. Oh troubled heart,
beset by now with volumes of regrets,
stop, read the sign some prophet planted

by the bridge, in bold black stenciled letters:
EVOLVE. A summary redemption promises
to wake the dead. Imagine them unfettered
by their sins. Our rosary of dreams, my dear
philanderer of air, ill-suits us for

what lies ahead: death's lidless eyes appraise
the broken record of our wanton days.
Time's apprentice to the past. Slowly the geese
assemble in a preordained formation.
So unlike us—they know their final destination.

*Askold Melnyczuk*

# Questions I Never Asked My Father

Do animals distinguish gender outside their own species?

Where is that book you once told me I should read, which
I had no time for?

For the last time, is dairy healthy or unhealthy?

How did you feel after getting that letter from your father
In which he called you a failure?

Do you regret bringing your mother over from the old country?

Did you mean what you said
About masturbation?

Why did you create the world?

How does death taste?

All I know is
I will be the winter now.

# Chorale: *In April*

**1**

Because pain is colloquial
as every true poem

because I can neither look nor entirely look
away

from myself

**2**

Two Lebanese boys on a stretcher—
fish in a net show more surprise.

**3**

I listen
for words rushing
from trees
through the April
staccato of rain:

a finite network of roots
wires the earth
and every caress
carries for thousands of miles.

4

Bewildering,
the mouths of the dead, methodically
stifling their hunger with flowers.

5

Soon these green fists
will open and the veins
of the leaves, hammered daily

by light, will swell until
the leaves themselves begin
to darken, shrivel, fall.

The living brother
must speak for himself.
The rain says nothing at all.

II.

# Late

**1**

to wake to the dark, misread the clock, think it
says five, sky between blinds black, turn again
to the pale green numbers and it's two-oh!-five,
you've slept an hour yet you're awake as though
a night and a day had passed

but this is the night and the day

**2**

in the eyepiece
of the camcorder
a woman wearing
mostly black,
black turtleneck
black pants,
walks quickly down
a city street
glistening
with rain.
Pan
to my face
reflecting the news
of her astonishing
departure.

We be what we be.

## 3

*being cut again and again*
*causes extreme pain,*
*so do not*
*be afraid*
*when the white pebbles*
*are being counted,*
*do not lie*
*and do not fear*
*the Lord of Death.*

*Since you are a mental body*
*you cannot die*
*even if you are killed*
*and cut up. You*
*are really the natural*
*form of emptiness, so*
*there is no need to fear.*

## 4

Like soft cotton swaying
the reeds
in Hellcat winter
gold. I think
it's Emma
Goldman
I've fallen for
each time:

a spirit that hisses:
*noli me tangere*

*Askold Melnyczuk*

## De Tocqueville in Newark

Already they were glowing, legendary:
Washington Street, The Little, McGovern's
where they kept the sea
on tap, the local history of rot.

That was the year you stood in church
reading John Donne, cursing
God and certain of the coward silence.
Kept waking under damp, shellacked

lilacs, a whirling in your head
like Wagner. Divinity
flowed through you. You kept moving.
Walked down streets paved by no blood

of yours, to parks no footsteps
you knew ever worried, or graveyards
where you scouted for familiar names,
knowing there too you'd be first.

Year of the Great Education, after
the power failure, a whole city
lit by the Collected Works
of Soren Kierkegaard. Year of the telluric.

That was the year she left you
for a boy named Rock. You stared
into the river on North Union.
You never finished *Werther*.

The Venus of Odesa

Returned then to the Empire of Lies
where everyone you knew was subject
and no one ever died of looting
of the lights, after the ice was born.

Tonight you have them back, the wired
streets, the strip joints
where you studied Greek or talked
to anyone

entirely inside your body
like never since.

*Askold Melnyczuk*

## La Bohème

Mimi, whose svelte
hands Rodolfo lipped
so hungrily last week,
can't climb

the stairs, and anyway
her cough
might break his epic
concentration on the work

where all
will be revealed:
heart, and more, laid bare.
God pulls,

snorting, toward
the pasture of the page.
Then, she's dying.
Death's homely spirit

wakens something human
in her friends.
Musetta prays.
Rodolfo hopes

they'll waltz again.
Then, of course, she's dead.
Rodolfo cries out:
*Mi-mi!*

THE VENUS OF ODESA

How every word
reveals us.
You begin with animal spirits
and a gift.

These you spoil early.
You begin with something luminous
soon lulled
into a little stupor.

Consider Montagato
who skins cats
for stews
in stylish kitchens;

Stanky, harvester
of dog-shit,
breeding worms
under his bed;

sweet Yvette, betrayed
by love, who wedges
into life
by peddling lemon peels

for oils and scents
that stimulate
the semi-
celibate Baudelaire,

Askold Melnyczuk

brooding, catatonic
in a louse-laced attic
on a dream in which
he's sailing

and although he's broke
and at her mercy,
nailed to the prow's
his mother's head.

It is the voyage
of a sailor damned
to scudding
seas aboard

a schooner in a bottle
where the rigging's spider-
sized; boat
that's whipped

and shaken by no tempest
but the senses
and the shapeless
self, which slips

one dawn
into a harbor
where a woman rises
from the water

The Venus of Odesa

like a Cytherian goddess
and the shore
is thick
with anxious men.

*Askold Melnyczuk*

## Poets' Loves

became our loves.
We pined
for Dora Markus
to embrace us;
yearned to hear
that shrill
invective scorch
the sullen south
once more.
Oh time! Stand still.

We outlined Olga's mouth;
took tea
with Valerie.
We wooed
Cassandra, who
was hung.
We dreamed Maud Gonne
slipped us the tongue.

But we were young.

# From the Streets

"Oh honey, what's that on your dress, oh
look, it's horrible, it's a tarantula, and

it's sucking on Jewish brains," shrieks
the woman pushing the cart through the Square.

Secular star in whorl above the kiosk, the ratty
sky rubbing earth. Nobody

sees. Anything. May be sunny,
may be raining fire. What happens, though,

when it gets really quiet? Who
do we hear? What is it goes

on and on inside, who pierces
the heart, center of light, with burning?

Names. I want names. Who listen to?
Why think some things belong to

poems, others not? The main question,
always on the edges, and burrowing, always

deeper, about love and depth, is it
ever asked right? Can a poor man love

*Askold Melnyczuk*

the obvious problems? Too rich. Where proceed?
Countdown: her I ... and she ... past

Endless mouths, brows, lobes....and souls?
Like the other day I found my Baltimore

Catechism, it said eyes shouldn't worship
strange etc., and marriage, a sacrament. And chastity.

So I knew I'd broken a few, between
friends. Understand then my shyness,

my shame. She I loved
who was married, I loved

any distance inside her, invisible
parks and waterfalls, the black

coca of eyes and hair, too, the wedded
knees and lonely chin, even if

not in love (and this for me not
the first this delicious problem), so

I ask, slyly, why still
hallucinating ways, and a woman, with whom

The Venus of Odesa

Sistine chapel of joys, too much, you think?
Like a flood in a citrine. But go back

obsessively, as is my way,
(your problem now) to her whom I she

the anonymous because
can it be

we so thoroughly hate
ourselves we hunger and chase

our own death exclusively, loving
what burns, and maims?

Self-dying, self-diluted, self-staining, we're
talking serious

rhetorical sprees, head and heart, deciding, since
who cares?

Stories on television, their uglier
errors, even so

the one whose eyes, round and dark
drew themselves into ovals, tears,

*Askold Melnyczuk*

other lips, another's eyes,
lozenges after loving,

something prior inside her smooched
to new life, who with

her humorous being could charm
a cactus, yet had something

desperate there, apparent in private
intensities. What is ambition,

soldiers in Crimea, what is desire?
How decide the shape our lives

take? The impossible language of God
and law ripped off by spiritual

busbies. Therefore the numinous
the night we lay on a human

bed on Linnaean, with human
time mark digitally

but were naturally elsewhere
space the endless, fingers locked, knee

## The Venus of Odesa

below knee, and flow
light in the dark. I never knew

how tears entered flesh,
no signs, like this is interesting

from a scientific perspective: I mean
does she hear me, speaking to her now?

Because I swear then 2,000 miles
whispered without telephones

and heard, perfectly, perfect
reception, and how escape

I only alive alone, and you
say: not our problem, hook

up with the passion (meaning: *suffer*)
of others, that's one way you know; another:

build a sepulchral city
of accounting tools, it will be

crowded with the shiny
tools of the age, it will feel

Askold Melnyczuk

strong, it will shine
like success and smell

sweetly of money, and you
will have to forgive it as something

men do
to get out of just such

a predicament, just, the either
whore question, that is anger,

no matter where it is aimed,
and which no one

said ends

# Head

Head mumbled to itself, so
I came nearer. We were by
the Lech Walesa Bridge
in Dorchester. I said

"I've loved …" It was floating
in the river, alone,
balding, with gray teeth, moth
wings stapled to its eyes,

and lips about to slip
into the stream.
"Which way …" it broke in,
rudely, and as often

in the past, I wished I had
a camera, so I
might later soberly reflect
on the hilarious

ambiguities of the moment—
"… to Ithaka?"

*Askold Melnyczuk*

# *The Odyssey:* Revised, Standard

**1**

Telemachus is watching MTV.


**2**

And when she sees him,
fierce, disheveled, bearded,
she crimps her mouth
and asks him to come back
in a couple of years, after
he has dealt with his anger, after
she has something
to compare him to.


**3**

And he agrees.
He bows.
Unstrings the bow.

There's nothing in the world
to rage at.
Athena grins benignly.
Zeus and Hera,
after years of counseling, done
fighting, tank
the clouds with pure ambrosia.

And little Eros never misses.

# On a Painting by Edward Kozak

*for Vika*

Swaying girls invite the dance:
Colors dress them, ribbons flow
(Wind, off canvas), in a trance
Shedding legacies of woe.

War upstages everything
You know. Little hermit, eat
A tank! Show your teeth. Pull
rank. Pull every string.

Become a legend. It will grow.
Defy the gods. Confuse the winds.
Bribe oceans. Harrow hell.
You did it all so well.

*Askold Melnyczuk*

## Simplon Pass

But that's the past, Head.

Like ten thousand
window sashes in a row:
that afternoon at Simplon Pass
fog lathering the mountain paths,
flecked with real edelweiss,
I thought the monastery
turned to smoke, when
a Saint Bernard, beast
of pure spirit, honoring
the saint who shut his eyes
to keep from falling
to the passing charms
of the bewitching, frail
Alps—cask bejeweling
his neck—slipped out
and I
remembered seeing for the first
time Father shaving.
And all history
etched in the glass
of these leaning
sashes, so the war,
venerable Head, came
as a desirable diversion,
distracting from
money fears, bad love.

# I. E.,

Everybody lives
on another planet.
Only you are here, with me.
Harrison Avenue. A community
fair brings out the ties and leather.

The years converge around
a meatgrinder on a stick,
tureen on a pedestal,
the rusting sleigh.

And you, after years,
drifting In and Away.

*Askold Melnyczuk*

# Sweet Enough

Astor Piazzolla
rakes the accordion, scoring
the other side

of tango,
it is that sweet
and hides a whip in it;

the cat stalks
summer in the window,
dynamite in the trees;

you leave again
for the south;
I worry.

When
this Christ air
shivers the room.

I lie still
under the lights
under the ceiling fan:

but to be
a disciple
is another thing—

THE VENUS OF ODESA

like music
becoming applause.
And I have known

that sensation
sweet enough
to kill time

I'll call Christ,
it is that light:
like, who

ever wanted to
hurt anyone, who
asked for it?

Not Tonita,
of Salvador
hurrying home

after bringing lunch
to her husband to nurse
her baby but the baby

with its brothers,
beg pardon, not them,
their torsos, were already sitting

*Askold Melnyczuk*

around the table,
heads on platters,
hands crowning

their skulls.
Where was the Jesus
feeling for her?

Can't say.
All I can:
a strange light

some people give off, from
and within
the heart, ceilings

lift, the pajaros
fly in, and the cat
in Christ himself

stirs awake, blinking
interest. For Tonita
this day was second

nature, she had already
dreamed it, lived
her whole

## The Venus of Odesa

life in grace
always knowing,
always sure

she owned nothing
but what the heart
could save in its fist:

so should we thank
our money
for helping this?

This not prosaic event.
This pure poetry
In our time? To write,

Love, is to remember,
is more. And not.
To write is to leave

Christ and Tonita
and you
entering the hieratic

privacies of the spirit
not easily named
or forgiven.

Askold Melnyczuk

# My Life Against the Berlin Wall

Martin, Thomas touched
the wound
like *colibri* beebalm:
better not to fly through glass!

And Abraham gave Isaac,
a story
I've never fully understood,
which makes it good,
and worth repeating.

The ties, invisible
silk cords binding us
to this earth
Able needed to escape from
are thinner than ever today.

And the Bible
stories oddly near
as I walk, encouraging
squirrels not to fall:
*pray keep your balance!*

on this Indian
Summer November Tuesday.
I wonder if they know
these days, being beautiful,
won't last, and will

THE VENUS OF ODESA

give way again
to the bureaucracies of ice
and protocols of snow.
But the myth
of the blue sky

seems more
than tale,
though you can't
touch it, package it, or keep it
going after dark

while what we know
of freedom hovers
bright under its tender
sway, the sweet
percussive nothingness

of faith. The frontier
of being is nothing
less than the next
breath, and yet
this listless eye

can't help not seeing
that the front's
not here, but further south,
because the skin
which breathes above the skin

Askold Melnyczuk

like an expansive fog, flowing
outward, south and east, and even
west, where they believe
they know the score, the skin
prickles and the sick

spirit sobs, feeling cut.
And so, maybe
I needed to see
just as when
slicing through
the carrot to

my thumb, I can't
keep from fingering
the flap of flesh,
so loose and tentative and there.
Faith it was

Walked up
and touched
a living God;
from then on knew
just what to do.

# The Cost of Nothing

Each morning I garden
I'm a whole man.
Even in the city.
The fucked-up city.

Tillandsia in the Ficus;
bromeliads in the fireplace;
even the fickle
Podocarpus thriving.

Once I would have done anything for you,
Poetry. Now I see how you treat us,
I say: fuck the work.
But if your friend needs you, drop everything.

*Askold Melnyczuk*

# Metamorphosis
### for Stuart

Some sickness broods above
this building like the clouds
that loose their scissored silks of snow
down Linnaean Street.

Everyone's sick.
Bewildered bodies quake
under a sickness that's the soul's
queer growth.

Latia down the hall
searing the couch, mind slurred
as the sky, may show
the sloughing

of a former self,
dream's fission: the teeth
of betrayal
tutoring the heart

until the lovely patient turns
to God, or death, or else
the death of God
which happens now and then.

She will awaken changed, become
her father and his chalk-cheeked
wife, spared
the vision, the violent

miracles, never
as vivid, as beautiful.

*Askold Melnyczuk*

# Nobody's Right

Red-winged blackbirds
must be mating.

Along the trail's top
in Hellcat Swamp

I watch them
pitching skyward.

\*

You know nine
of ten swans
mate for life?

I love the ones
who dive
apart, rehearsing.

\*

My fingers rioting
against the page—

the obvious stuff,
you on top with your shirt off

shining, the sea
ungirdled.

# The Light Around You

Cowshit Corners, Maine.
Where else?

I hardly thought then
that was the peak.

Crest heaving crest,
Sea and snowdrift.

We crest, fall, mostly
Fall. Piebald
crescent moonlight.

      Not about me.

      Not about you.

I don't remember.

There was no getting
from there to here.

A truck treading ice
on a lake I don't
know the name of.
Smoke in the pines.

Never ask about this
again, not about

the porcelain doll,
the suicidal cactus,
Zapatenku, again.

Never.
By the lake you said you smiled
for the camera
because your face was crooked.

There was always a light
around you, though.

Only, the colors
kept changing: from

green, to blue, to red.

# Haruspicating Clouds in Cambridge

Inside this old world
winter, the streets' habitués
resplendent in the wild

colors of discarded clothes—
fuchsia shirts hoisted above
golf green synthetics, refuse

from someone's Caribbean cruise—
become conspicuous as palms
in snow, inside a cold

that is the country's current weather:
no gulf breeze
wings our scarves and our charities

wither like marigolds, while
trees curse the incurable
and tactless winter turning

branches vulnerable.
It is the old anxiety one feels
while walking, reading, or with friends:

*What is the meaning of* ... etcetera ...
I've learned the anglo-saxon blush
before the high-blown noun.

*Askold Melnyczuk*

That was a decade for the dead
to bide their time: Jean Donavan
will find a voice among

the still dazed young
who caterwaul along the Caligari
shadows of their fathers'

nightmares and the scorned
be canonized as saints
and celebrated by the sons

and daughters of the ones
who thought them fodder
yet asked schools to bring back prayer.

Years ago, my parents traveled
back to see the camps
that prospered on their youth.

My father's now collecting stamps
Who once watched men in brown
Slap his old man around.

He stares at this,
All this,
And laughs.

# Alley Cat

*for TS*

You might have liked
burning a city

had you been human. Mustard Coat.
Mink Skin. Little Genghis.

Bred on thin bones,
slop of new money,

but loved by your mother
who guzzled the afterbirth,

you wasted your youth
on squirrels.

Dreamed of roadkill, sparrows
reamed on a spit.

Knowing by hurt what happens
when a creature crosses a road

at just the wrong moment,
you duck any friend.

You might have blinded a giant.
Loved a dark goddess.

Seen men raiding the wallet
of a sleeping, one-legged man.

*Askold Melnyczuk*

Watched white boys
take out the trash.

And take her and take her.
What is the soul of an audience?

Instead, sweetness, you found
your way here.

Up these long stairs.
Into these peeling rooms:

Books, trizub, figs.
Let yourself go

to my ministrations.
Oh my little eunuch.

My frank odalisque.
Changed from that monster of needing

in what filthy corner
will you be the day

that feathery engine
finally stops?

# The Great Feeding

They gather at the troughs, in the gutters,
the city animals, and more
from heaven come, with wings and no wires
actually walking, and breathing:
because desire is merciless, they appear
with bird bodies and the faces of the poor
on farms and on Mondays
stalking the streets for something to slake
their wanting every mere, every fertile,
every torn branch and blown flower,
every hour not filled or borne
by a joy who squared the job of the lilies,
task of ant, clematis' duty,
a longing greater than God's
the day He retired and His children
shaped this city on a hill,
a swamp, in history,
burying arrows yet beautiful
under the arc-lamp of moon;
who wanted a federal paradise got a feral,
the halyards and winches in the harbor
hoisting not manna but tea, coffee, coke—
cats and gargoyles, harpies, oil
Pegasus, sick dogs, magnates
of faith, and they eat
the rubber tires, and the flakes of neon.
They eat it all. And they have it, too.

*Askold Melnyczuk*

## Poem

February Sunday shielding
eyes from sun

naming waves
Helen Ruth Johanna

snow blends
with surf spray

wind carried
wind breathing

brown slant
fence behind

trembles, hiss of sand
gulls

I know these waves

you are not among them

# Goya's Winter

*for Beatra*

### I

There is a dog who barks
against the wind and whiteness

and, looking up, becomes
a solitary witness
to his world

### II

of hooded men
who might be magi

but are hunters
gaunt and cowled
against the weather;

### III

one
lean tree
that's blown
and gleaming
down
the suck of wind

## IV

nowhere a hint
of angels;

## V

only a hog
draped whole
over a meditative mule.

## VI

Behind, the torso
of a lake
under the shadow
of a mountain,
bluish spectre
of the unconceived
Cezanne.

## VII

Moreover,
earth and sky.

## VIII

A world,
hungry, doing
what it must
in order
to appease
the body,
trudging,
willful,
toward what once,
without a hit of irony,
we called *the light*.

## IX

All this
and more we cannot see
the dog alone
takes in

and bares his teeth.

Askold Melnyczuk

# Melancholy Baby

Join the March
wind flicking the nude
oak: enter
the leeched minarets
of the grass, the soaked
sigh of stunned
flesh slowly
turning, as after
love, while
the adulterous starlings,
sing down the sun
off-key adieus, and the last
snow lingers like
the memory of promise
stayed by the breath of others,
though your own hands reached out
to trace a lineage once felt accessible
as air, drawn from the wind, from a world
where Walden seasoned the Ganges, and wheat
battened on blood—pull back
from this new season
sheltering always
and ever more beautiful
lusts, the same
still, from all
you've seen, touched, dreamed, remembering
"who maketh the darkness his convert …"
What's sightless eyes us best
and from the syllables of things
we're made a living speech

THE VENUS OF ODESA

to testify we're seen.
Admit to the stones they know
more than you, and are you.

Askold Melnyczuk

## Prayer of Origin

Pinochet, a close reader
of the Tao
says to himself:

*You have been a fire, now
try being a river.*

I would like to be a river a while:
the Yellow River, racing
over the bones of Li Po
or the Dnipro, singing past
Kaniv and Chernobyl,
or the Charles, swaggering
down the oasis of dawn.

Even Pinochet learns in the afterlife.

After life, out of the pastoral
yeast, I will never rise
again. I will never

leave, because, love,
I am the reckless elk
leaping across the highway

and I will be the lost horses
of Ipswich, and the marshes
on Plum Island in a drizzle
and the easel
on which the sky rested.

THE VENUS OF ODESA

And our first kiss.
And our last.

Askold Melnyczuk

# After a Snowfall the Second Day of Spring

*for Gus and Eiko*

What else are we here for?
The unfinished lives, the garages
uncleaned, love
letters unsent,
filled with complaints,
arguments with the mysteriously
missing beloved who knows
why she's here no better than we.
The projects half
started, novels and plays,
the efforts at politics, the partial
despair at how close we come
before falling, the friendships
that promise deliverance and maybe
come nearest of all to delivering
what they promised, the unvisited
cities, the grackles
unseen in our yards, the secret
life of the soil glimpsed only
on television, the planets
dismissed with a shrug and some lies
about science, parents unknown
the mothers and fathers mysterious
in their own homes, and to each other,
the endless talks with ourselves,
and no answers, just
stutters, then spring

# Cambridge Typewriter Is Now in Arlington

Crossing the Lech Walesa Bridge in Dorchester
I think: what we want is a reliable place
amid the apparent cultural incoherence.

For example, this postcard: La Virgen, Reina
y Madre del Carmelo entrega el escapulario
a San Simon Stock. AD XVII no less.

Did they really see these angels once,
floating heads of cherubim unmistakable
in the chiaroscuro, the lute players

and barefoot minstrels, sweetly piping
sexless floating beings enfolded
in the dark robes of the Mother, bambino

on knee, a crown held aloft by a couple
of sad-faced, distinctly feminine winged humanoids?
If the world fails to swathe us in ermine

or synthetic, suggesting thereby we're unworthy
of our lives, and the attention we think we've paid
to things, think about the Lech Walesa Bridge,

whose history the next generation won't forget
because they never knew it. Her eyebeams
are visible, Alex. We see her gaze

*Askold Melnyczuk*

and feel it and it creates a cluster
of heads like grapes. Once someone
understood that vision. Yea, though I study

pretty hard, and believe in belief, I worry
it might be a cartoon. I sit here unable
to explain this important thing, composing instead

an a cappella to the typewriter repair man.

# III.
Personae

## Girl in the Prado

> *And humanity is like a young girl bursting with longing ...*
> —Unamuno

My feet are sore, and so
is my spirit, from so
much to see. Like this Greco
with his people braiding into

fire, the relentless
bodies, stalks and nettles
or weird-colored flames, his
world as far as Cadiz

from the things I know.
This is not shopping. No
Straw hats, flowers, or zapatos.
What should I do

with what I see?
That boy near
the fat woman—
the dark one

in tight jeans,
black eyes, full lips:
I saw him before at
*The Garden of Earthly Delights*

*Askold Melnyczuk*

where the Bosch-God, hidden
in the canvas, tortured sin-
ners for their
indiscrete desires.

Surrounded by saints, why
do I feel he's
asking me to choose?
My father, the minister,

told me I couldn't
keep "the ecstasy
of faith" alive
without prayer and good

works. He said the body
was like Chinese mountains
lunging upward, to the sky.
I would like to be

seven again, and riding
bareback by the streams
on my grandfather's farm,
Medellin's mountains drowsing

in twilight, and knowing
my sister and mother
stood in the kitchen
preparing pescado, setting

THE VENUS OF ODESA

plates, their laughter stirring
the air, drifting
through the farmhouse
braiding with orchids and leaves

under the crowded sky.

Askold Melnyczuk

# The Revelation of Julius Caesar

*Omnia Gallia est ... et cetera ...*
Lord, the rockweight of history
my little whores—
I write as I ride, compose
in my sleep, and drive you all
into the tapestry of my dream
and look:
like puppets you dance
to my song of blood.

You do not know the game.
You do not know the rules.

I am of no one but God.

This is for those
who do not believe
in the mysteries:

Ages ago, in a garden
—I was alone and in love—
a voice in my head
spoke of divinities
of the gods and demigods
and it said I
was of their number.
It told of the brevity
and hours of earth
and commanded: Go down
into the arcades of hell.

THE VENUS OF ODESA

And I went—
into the hell of the heart—
and heard the howl of Cerberus
and knew the elaborate horrors
of which the poets sang

and I went beyond these
to a place without mildness
in the mind all excitement
where was nothing but light.

There I strayed briefly
—what living being can bear heaven?—
and I heard the commotion and flutter
of stars
and saw before me the choices.

I knew then the world was mine
and whatever I dreamed I would make

and for that I gave up His palace.

Then, like an eagle of light
I rose to my fate

and the blood came in blankets.

And before my death
the horses wept
and the birds cried: Love me!

*Askold Melnyczuk*

# Descartes: Final Notes

(In February 1650, Descartes succumbed to the harsh Scandinavian winter while instructing Queen Christina in philosophy.)

I am not wind nor the mists
that haunt the palace gardens
like a gown without a woman.

I am not the hoarse voice
whispering:

>What is the difference between body
>and body?

>What pain grows in the halls
>behind my eyes?

>What is a circle?

Sunlight freezes on the pillow.
What can I know?

# Dear Liv Ullman, I Hope You Are Never Unhappy

Dear Liv Ullman, I suppose you know
I have seen all of your pictures.
They haunt me when I am alone
in bed and not watching television.

Dear Liv Ullman, there is beauty
in travel. It is not easy to live
in America all the time. It is not simple
to leave, either. Will you advise me?

Dear L.U., I am glad you ignored
my first two letters. They embarrass me
with their shallowness: please burn them.
Writing to someone famous is hard.

Dear Liv, Great News! Soon I am sailing
on a ship to Sweden to become
an actor. I do not speak Swedish.
This will be my last letter.

Dear Liv Ullman, this will be my last
letter. I speak now English
with a Swedish accent. White nights are all
I remember, and the cold, and your eyes.

*Askold Melnyczuk*

# Swan Song

I was never beautiful.
I learned by heart the octaves of grief
and the peculiar phrases of a man's desires.
Mine was the chord seldom struck. Oh
they gave me an arm to walk
over the esplanade. I walked
with the arm. They stood
near the edge, watching,
humming the ruse of the borrowed car
and from their pockets rose the *petite chanson*
of the hungry key. I walked on alone
and the water came, touched my feet, and was gone.

The water grew darker
over the years. One night
I asked, for the peace of my soul,
for the hell of it,
what, Plato, is "the life of the mind?"
I thought I knew it, thought I lived it.
Why do I wonder then
what it is to be a "light
and winged thing" or to whirl
in the queer ether of perfect form?
I have never found the everlasting loveliness
which neither comes
nor goes.

    And I asked Catullus
how it was with the flesh.
Could I have liked a gambol in the rosebush

or saying with my body
the wordless prayer, curving
back, going on my knees
in homage?
"You are a vine in a barren field
that cannot climb by its own strength...."
No. I was a woman. Whole.
So what if I signed my name only
in a soft white sand
the sea would soon broom out?

My dears, I do not love destruction
but the self walking alone
is a vulnerable radiance.
It should know splendor or make its confession
to the grass, and the stars
and move on.

# IV.
## Versions from the Ukrainian

Three Fables by Hrihory Skovoroda (1722–1794)

# Owl & Thrush

As soon as they noticed Owl, the other birds started razzing her.

"Aren't you bothered," asked Thrush, "That for no crime of yours they abuse you? Doesn't it worry you?"

"Not in the least," she replied softly. "They do the same among themselves. As for the nuisance, I bear it because, though Crow, Rook, and Magpie may slander, Eagle and Horn-Coot and the citizens of Athens esteem me."

Gist: It's better to be understood and loved by one intelligent, copious soul than by a thousand fools.

## Dogs

Two dogs lived in one yard.

One day a stranger passed by their gate.

The larger dog sprang up and barked until the fellow disappeared. He then settled back into his cove under the lindens.

"What did you get out of that?" the other dog asked.

"Kind of boring just sitting here …"

"Not all strangers are our master's enemies," the smaller dog continued. "If he had been, you think I'd have sat silently by? A dog's life isn't bad, but to howl without reason? What's that about?"

Gist: The wise know what to censure; fools prate without purpose.

# Eagle and Magpie

Magpie said to Eagle: "Tell me, tornado of feathers, don't you tire of tracing gyres in the sky all day, as though stuck on the thread of a screw?"

"I'd never come down," replied Eagle, "if bodily needs didn't force me."

"And I'd never leave the city," said Magpie, "if I were Eagle."

"Neither would I," smiled Eagle, "if I were Magpie."

Gist: Those made to play with eternity are happier in fields, orchards, and groves than in cities.

*Askold Melnyczuk*

## Five by Taras Shevchenko

# And the Sky

remains unwashed, and the waves
                         sleep;
    reeds bend in no wind
like drunks.
    My god!
How long will I keep
boring the waves
from inside
    this open prison?

God's mum
As the fields
    of yellowing grass.

He'll never tell the truth.

But there's no one else to ask.

THE VENUS OF ODESA

# Fine By Me

Fine by me if I live here
             or not;
if any of you,
strangers,
remember me,
 or not.
It's all the same to me.

A slave among strangers,
      with no one
to mourn me:
      that's how I'll die.

And I'll take everything with me.

I won't leave a trace
      in this country that's not
ours anyway.

Here no father dares to teach
      his son or say:
                *Pray.*
*Pray for him. He died for us.*

It's all the same to me
if that kid prays or not.

*Askold Melnyczuk*

What's not all right with me
is if
      the bastards
      drug the girl
and set the house on fire
and she wakes up to find
she's robbed.

No way
      that flies with me.

# Never Marry Rich

Never marry rich—
She'll chase you from her door.
Never marry poor—
You'll sleep in a ditch.

Marry the wind instead.
What will be, will be;
If naked, then, naked.
This way, none will fuss,

Or try to cheer you up,
Or ask: What hurts,
My precious? Where?
No one will care.

They like to say misery
Seeks company.
Don't believe it. Better
Keep it to yourself. Forever.

*Askold Melnyczuk*

# For Gogol

In our literary hive:
words piled on words.
One chokes the heart,
The other tears it apart,

Yet God's not said a word.

    Who will I show this poem to,
    Who will welcome
    This new language of ours?

    Everyone's deaf, asleep,
    In chains…and who cares?
    You laugh, I weep,
    My grand friend.

    What fruit
Do our tears bear?
Strange fruit, brother.
Freedom's canons
Won't echo across Ukraine.
No father will ever surrender
His son for honor's
Sake, neither for
Glory, nor for freedom.
He won't cut him down.

No, he'll fatten him
And, later, sell him
To a Moscow butcher.

Let it be, brother.
You'll laugh; I'll weep.

*Askold Melnyczuk*

# Fragment

To turn a rich man's mill
Wheel, water will
Flow uphill.

The poor man
Living in a valley
Never finds the well.

# War

*after Pavlo Tychyna*

Alone last afternoon, I fell asleep.
I dreamed a son—lovely to imagine.
Then as happens in a dream,
I lost control. I thought I heard the screen

door slam. No. It was a gun.
We stood on a battlefield—and me in my apron!
Fingers to lips, we crept to a cypress.
Came the angry dance of fire and smoke, and then

we were on an island. I said to my bright
boy: "Guess we'll have to go soon, to fight
the enemy." And he said: "There
is no enemy, mother. Never was, never

will be. The only tyrant is here, in the heart."
I stared at him hard, wondering how he got so pure.
He said: "Wish me luck. I'm off to find the cure."
I didn't understand. His words made me start.

"The cure for human madness. But it might take time...."
When I woke, the radio whispered, and the moon was up.

*Askold Melnyczuk*

## Two by Mykola Rudenko

# The King of Tasmania

> Most of the aboriginal population of Tasmania was wiped out by
> British colonists in the 19th century

I am he. I am the last. That means I'm king.
There's still a Tasman Sea, and a Tasmania.
A country must have a king.
This is the part I was sentenced to play.

Every crown rests on bones. Not for medals
will I raise this sepulcher of skulls
but to record how they suffered—my people.
These skull I snatched from the dogs.

From the dogs, the trees ... Study the gardens:
each apple-tree lapped native blood.
They slew us for fertilizer, certain
our bodies nourished sweet fruit. A bargain.

There's no more fertilizer. I gather bones
for my pyramid. Awful.
Soon I'll sit higher than the tallest trees.
I, the king, below me, my people.

Wherever I turn I find foreign money.
The only familiar souls are the fleet kangaroos.
In them, ancestors rise. When I die
we'll meet again in green furrows.

The Venus of Odesa

Even now, foreigners race to my country
to poach on our fields, dig up our gardens.
I'll play the Customs Man bribed by their gin.
The worship of kings, don't they know, is a duty.

To them I seem mad. That's nothing new.
My pyramid grows, and it grows.
There's a sacred prophecy I pursue:
a tower will outlast the empire.

Though my people are gone, the faith
of the fathers and grandfathers survives:
who hopes for swelled harvests from corpses
reaps nothing but corpses on corpses. Then, dies.

*Askold Melnyczuk*

# Spring

No delight in the riot of trees
Sweeping green slopes and groves:
Young, I counted too many
Of them rising from graves.

Green we sank to the earth,
Wounded, not pleading with killers.
Boys matured into maples.
Inside poplars, girls whispered.

No delight in the sprouting of shoots:
I know what nourished the roots.
I'll order the nightingale
To publish my griefs.

Let her drink the waters of dawn,
In her throat refine them to song—
And all that followed my autumn
Rehearse to a late-blooming youth.

## Two by Marjana Savka

# from *A Short History of Dance*

Listen, child, to a wise old wolf:
in dance, everything has its own meaning.
Here we've stopped—
we haven't touched,
yet our breath dances to one rhythm,
always stronger and faster.
We began with the foxtrot—but do you hear the pulse of tango?
For another minute, listen to the vibrations in silence.
Now, hold out your palm,
let's find the pressure points,
here our history begins:
from here rush rivers
of mania,
a yellow heat flares
in the ruby eyes of longing,
firing a reckless tarantella in the veins.
If you dare, go all the way to the end on wire bridges
above the boiling lava.
I promise everything—
to dance with you,
to be with you in the dance,
be inside you on far alpine peaks,
in blinding green fields,
black chasms,
in the folios of Egyptian libraries,
on red silk scrolls in Chinese shops,
everywhere and anywhere,
amid the beads, amid the sands,

on cinnamon waves,
in the pleated water-lilies,
on whispering sheets,
tangling time and space.
… later, though, don't pretend
you didn't want exactly this.…

# My God Spends All Night

My god spends all night forming his battalions,
Is a crack shot, wages wars.
My god forgives my curses
As he polishes his stones.
My god won't hide behind my back,
Throws quilted covers over children.
My god buys tourniquets
Then lines up to give blood.
My god can't get a good night's sleep
While the entire country's standing guard.
My god allows me never to forgive
And lets me call things as they are.

V.

# Vermont

Once his soul slipped out, hiding
in corral slime, cedar tips, raspberry
clumps, glazing the sourwood—

and everything glanced back:
white pine   birch   moss-crusted rock

kingdom of flickering whips

and no distance between
and all because he prayed
for the resurrection

of his bestial nature

*Askold Melnyczuk*

## Downer Forest Road

A fox lopes past
beebalm the blurred
hummingbird translates
from flower to flying.

Bearded trees
dream of rain.
Here, appetite recovers
simplicity. Moss

releases a shimmering.
The skin
above the skin
shivers, remembering

earlier gardens:
the rural aurora
sunk in the blood.
Row after

row of corn,
peppers, onions;
the daylilies' habit
of dying

one mouth to open
another. Earth,
I want to learn
how the mustard seeds,

THE VENUS OF ODESA

small as the sins
of a boy, know
to break into green.

*Askold Melnyczuk*

# Buddhist Diary: 1954–2024

# Great Blue Heron

Not the flapping of sheets in a gale
hook of neck
tucked in the breast
beak like bone straws
scythes for wings

not its crooked indifference
as it cuts
with something like purpose
across the sky

over a man on the crest
of a hill

and refuses to look
at the small being stunned
by the stately motion
who half expects
next to emerge
from the green
huddled pines
the mammoth
the saber tooth

who cannot see
for the life of him how
he connects to these worlds

who knows
the fear of the other

*Askold Melnyczuk*

of the close life
eyes blinking
hiding a hope
shaped like a prayer:

that what gives life
to the bird
nestle around him
gather him too

# A Trophy of Shadows

And when the hunters shot her son, killing him instantly, she looked back only once, and kept loping toward the acacias where her own prey cowered behind the yellowing blades. The ark of the covenant was cut from acacias; Romans used them for a crown of thorns.

She sees it all: the vulture circling the body; the forest of gazelles on which she'll graze till blood and meat restore her; even the fish swarming her muzzle when at last she falls into the river, done with flight. In the end, who escapes? Her final triumph: crocs will shred the pelt so coveted by the humans. Because what we love we become; what we hate we already are.

Askold Melnyczuk

# Who

> *The wall that separates today from tomorrow must be torn down
> so that tomorrow could be yesterday again.*
> —Paul Celan

Who stamped your ticket
at the door has gone

You've heard the screams
at night, had dreams
of orange flumes, the flames

a holiday display

Andalusia in your eyes

oh desperate conjuring,
a debonair
inflection parsing sin

(where many of our joys begin)

but words, unmoored, swarm
summer air like swifts
above a meadow

where I, half dreaming, rock
in aftershock

the seismic ahistorical
yet utterly corporeal, aligns:

## The Venus of Odesa

You, dead. A
war. *Pregunta*:

how
split an atom
in the heart
to make the world whole?

what wonder that our knowledge
(the clichés we learned in college)

allowed us not to know

Fat Boy, Dresden, Kramatorsk

so much more

a vessel, tempest-tossed

Ahoy!

No Ithaka in sight

Declare a fire at the core
of yearning

and our loss

Askold Melnyczuk

# In the Arms of the World

When I fell into the arms of the world
I requested the wind:

*Blow through the bones
Of the dead, blow
Down the hollow
Sockets and rims of the skulls*

*Blow down rivers
Of tears, blow
The uprising sand
So invested*

*In dying, but never assume
I am not furious.
Live for the sparrows
Who know*

*There's a con
In all concepts.
They demand, I obey.
Demand sunlight:*

*I open the sky.
Worms—unzipper the earth.
Demand dawn. Demand
Dusk. Demand peace*

## The Venus of Odesa

*Which, alas, is never*
*On offer. Instead,*
*Ink the lips, slip on lace;*
*Draw the blinds;*

*Hazard of grace,*
*Beg the birds*
*To honor your pain.*
*Sleep in the rain,*

*Certain what's mended*
*Must break again.*
*O, mother, reborn*
*A bird in Buddha's*

*Lap outside Pemberton*
*Market, when*
*You stood on the rim*
*Of the world*

*You paced out seven strides, saying:*
*I am supreme in this world*
*Into whose arms you have fallen.*
*I have brought you*

*That you might embrace*
*Every wound, every crevice*
*Every ember of doubt*
*And never hope to get out.*

*Askold Melnyczuk*

# Portrait of Lucie at Stop and Shop

Hesitant high heels
tottering, nimble-nosed
fawn on an errand

for her mother who
once nipped her hind
for burrs, then

urged her: Go!
Go to the people's temple
to testify that everybody's lost.

The lambs are led to slaughter
by a shepherd who's insane.
Oh my dear! So what if your

fluorescent hair
has not been cut this century?
*Grow into one of us*, I urged.

You smiled:
*I'd rather die.*
Then, did.

# The Other Lives

I don't know much about the other lives—
the ones before, or to come, or contiguous
in which I'm Nero, the moral null,
the Queen's astronomer prophesying war,
or evening's snake that slithers
from the horse's skull
and bites king Oleg in the leg.
Did apples smell as red?
Will days at the Carpathians still fall
with every unripe drift
of macadam, or misplayed note
of *Alley Cat*, while Artie shakes his head?

In Ryegate, dirt roads lock
like chains ringing hills
and rustic lines of rock
bind farm and meadow,
while runic lanes inside the brain,
mapping the wild topography
of thought, the fields
irrigated by a lunar rain,
encourage travelers to take
every turn there is to take
and I am grateful
to have strayed this far into the earth.

At twenty-three, I threw off
my jacket and shirt and sat
half-naked in the middle
of Massachusetts Avenue, singing

a *Marseillaise* of loss and rage.
Cops attended the audition.
The day was sunny, the wine French.
How to address that boy from here?
Answer that anthem.
A mist glides up the hill, over the open
earth, enveloping the sanguine
tanager perched inside

a green café, and over
webs shimmering
like something fallen from the sky.
This is how it must be to be kissed
by a deer in a dream; like love
before the havoc of the past cuts loose
in a kitchen rage; a wisp of truce
until the Indians and the French
descend again on Deerfield, dragging
prisoners up Bayley-Hazen Road
to Canada, where time
distills their children into barkeeps, cooks.

Dawn of webs. Dropped limp
from pines, cocooning spears
of apple trees, rayed taut
between the maples' branches,
sprayed over grass
in crippled stars, in targets, startled mouths, moons
drunken o's, mandalas, the ouroboros,
wheel of samsara turning …

## The Venus of Odesa

They clutch at my face
as I walk out of the mist
that's burning in the sun.

Askold Melnyczuk

## All Talk Is Moths

*for Alex*

I nestled among pines
beside a toad whose journey
I interrupted, and curled my arms
around my legs, and stared
at the trees. Then I took out
a thermos and poured a cup
of coffee. A moth fell in
and it was too late to save it.

Twilight.
You, deepening around me.

Not that I forgot
debts to society, or friends
and the usurious interest we pay.

Not that I forgot
hearts mangled like syntax
by strangers

or years speaking
only in fragments.

But here I was anyway, drinking
a moth's wing
happy past speech.

# The Venus of Odesa

*On a clay model of the Polovtsian Baba,*
*a pagan burial figure resembling*
*the Venus of Willendorf*

Transfixed, obedient
gray clay imperfectly glazed,
utterly sated at last:

the future of the world
once burned
under your lids.

Never, woman, no
man's, will
you find another to

love you
as he did,
does—love

being a life-
long, death-
long conversation—

loves you
as a god
might love the river

where I walk—
millennia, or days
gone by

Askold Melnyczuk

like water
(does the water know?)—
that's how

it sometimes is—
particular, disinterested
and friendly to the geese—

and nothing
careless in the taste
of air on clay

or tongue.
The idiocy of blood
and ideology

of bone
don't fool
you now.

I hold you at arm's length.
I touch you with my thumb.
I hope

The flesh this was knew
every crevice, every rain—
and did it know

THE VENUS OF ODESA

how far a man may go
to raze his father's house,
crawl home?

Askold Melnyczuk

# Verses from Shantideva

*for Geshe Tsulga (1939–2010)*

Where will I find leather enough
To cover the earth?
Yet, wearing leather-soled shoes
Have I not done it?

*

Impossible
To control external events;
Yet if I tame my own mind,
Do I need to?

*

We dwell
In the presence of
The Buddhas and Bodhisattvas
Who see all.

*

Spawned by my own actions,
My enemies.
It's thanks to me
They're in hell.

*

Free awhile?
Give up frowning and anger.
Smile.
Be a friend and counsel to the world.

# Big Thanks

My profound gratitude to Marc Vincenz and his good team at Mad Hat for giving this book a life.

Thanks and thanks to the friends who helped with the shaping of this manuscripts and to the editors who published many of these poems. A writer's solitary work is always stimulated by vitalizing conversations with fellow-practitioners. Over the years I've been incredibly fortunate to have known and shared work with Stuart Dischell, Steven Cramer, Tom Sleigh, Peter Balakian, Sven Birkerts, Martin Edwards, Marie Howe, Ha Jin, Rosanna Warren, Fanny Howe, Lara Stecewycz, Steven Ratiner, Thomas Sayers Ellis, Liam Rector, Lloyd Schwartz, Bill Corbett, Fred Marchant, David Ghitelman, Thomas O'Grady, Eric Hoffman, George Starbuck, Diana Der Hovanessian, Derek Walcott and Seamus Heaney. My sister, the painter and children's book author, Hanna Melnyczuk-Stecewycz, has always inspired me by her devotion to her art. But it was my mother's passion for poetry that started it.

And to Alex, love and gratitude for everything and always.

# Acknowledgments

Some of these poems first appeared in:

*Agni*
*The Alaska Quarterly*
*The American Poetry Review*
*Arts Fuse*
*The Boston Globe*
*The Boston Phoenix*
*Boulevard*
*Caliban*
*Denver Quarterly*
*Graham House Review*
*Grand Street*
*HAGL*
*Lily Poetry Review*
*MSS*
*The Nation*
*The New Yorker*
*Partisan Review*
*Pequod*
*Poetry*
*Ploughshares*
*Snail's Pace Review*
*Times Literary Supplement*

"The Sky's Unwashed" appeared in *The New Yorker*.

"Dance of the Tomahawks" appeared in *The Village Voice*.

"Late" appeared in *The American Poetry Review*.

"Chorale: In April," "The Sunday Before Easter," "The Usual Immigrant Uncle Poem," "The Way of the World," and "After a Snowfall" first appeared in *Poetry* (Chicago).

"The Voyagers," "The Usual Immigrant Uncle Poem," and "The Sunday Before Easter," appeared in *Under 35: The New Generation of American Poets* (Doubleday).

"Girl in the Prado" first appeared in *The Nation* and was reprinted in *The Longwood Anthology of Modern Poetry*.

"The Enamel Box" appears in *The McMillan Anthology of Poetry*.

"The Sunday Before Easter" appears in *Ukrainian Poets Respond to the War*.

# About the Author

ASKOLD MELNYCZUK has published four novels, a book of stories, and a novella about the life of Rimbaud. *What Is Told* (Faber, 1994), a *New York Times* Notable, was the first commercially published novel to highlight the Ukrainian refugee experience. Other novels include an *LA Times* Best Books of the Year, and an Editor's Choice by the American Library Association's Booklist. A volume of selected non-fiction, *With Madonna in Kyiv: Why Literature Still Matters (More than Ever)* will be published in 2026 by Harvard. He edited a book of essays on the St. Lucian Nobel-prize winning poet Derek Walcott and is co-editor of *From Three Worlds*, an anthology of Ukrainian writers from the 1980s generation. He's the recipient of a Lila Wallace Award in Fiction, the George Garret Award from AWP, and awards from the Massachusetts Cultural Council in fiction, poetry, and non-fiction. His work has appeared in *The New Yorker*, *The Paris Review*, *The Gettysburg Review*, *The Missouri Review*, *The Times Literary Supplement* and elsewhere. Founding editor of *Agni*, for which he received the PEN-Magid Award for Editing, and Arrowsmith Press, he has taught at Boston University, Harvard, Bennington College and currently teaches at the University of Massachusetts–Boston.

www.ingramcontent.com/pod-product-compliance
Lightning Source LLC
Chambersburg PA
CBHW020333170426
43200CB00006B/366